The Lady Poetic Principle Volume 2

The Second Volume of Hip-Hop Inspired Poetry and Lyrics

by Lady Poetic

First edition.

Lady Poetic. The Lady Poetic Principle Volume 2

Social and Music Links:

https://soundcloud.com/lady-poetic

https://ladypoetic.bandcamp.com/music

https://www.instagram.com/ladypoetic9/

https://www.facebook.com/ladypoeticLP

https://www.youtube.com/@LadyPoetic09

This book is dedicated to every person who has supported my art.

Foreword:

Since the release of The Lady Poetic Principle in 2023, I have been on an incredible journey and written thousands of bars along the way! Behold the latest edition in the Lady Poetic Poetry Collection!

After joining The Temple of Bars hip-hop podcast as a co-host, along side the main host and my long time comrade and creative partner, Wilkshake, I delved more into recording and releasing music again, starting with The Lady Poetic Mixtape Vol. 1 which released July 19th 2024. Included within this compilation are lyrics from that album, as well as from several single songs and lyrics from collaborations throughout 2024 and 2025.

On Pi Day (3.14) of 2025, I released the Storyteller's Page EP (within one minute of a lunar eclipse!), a collection of 6 brand new and rather brilliant songs highlighting my love of storytelling in hip-hop. I also re-recorded and added Timid Wild One as a bonus track (you may recall reading that one in the first poetry volume), and made an intro track compiled out of previous storytelling rhyme snippets. Those lyrics are shared within this book as well.

On another note, I was asked several times over the last year or two to write obituary poems, to be read at funerals of loved ones. I respectfully share those in this volume as well.

Thank you, dear reader, not only for reading this book, but for reading *a* book, and keeping the art of book-reading alive. This for you, for other artists, and for the love of poetry and hip hop. Peace and blessings to you and enjoy my second published book of poetry, The Lady Poetic Principle Volume 2!

Love, LP

3

Contents:

Single Song Lyrics, Collaborations, Poems and More:

6

Amnesia (From the Infinity Files)

I'm on an enigmatic safari
Surviving like an AIDS patient on Biktarvy
Grapplin' with gangrene of the soul
It's cold- so is my coffee
Swimming in marine imagery- Guy Harvey
Marveling at sea serpentry, never sorry
Hand feed me unpoisoned dates, crepes and calamari
Draping windows to the world with finely threaded saris
The starry skies, opening up to Ares on the rise
Parting clouds poured out rounds of angels singing lies
Size it up, grab a cup, overflow, never enough
Half empty, half full
Draw the line, surface still
Working wordsmiths for the thrill
Swallowing pride like a jagged little pill
Polar opposites repelling magnet poles, sniffles, chills
The realest underneath it all, to find us is a search
Amnestic but the best is when we celebrate our worth!

Night (From the Infinity Files)

The content creator, greatest showman officiator
Obstinate mayor, hesitating for a favor
Subterranean professionals positing majors
Players cherry picked, then climbing up the stairs
One way to go but every vantage point is different
Forcing poise and growth then candidly admit it
Portray who wants the most, then add this to revisit
Storybooks with pages worn and bindings frail and rigid
It's frigid and cold, out on limbs growing old
Like memories of yesterday, an Outkast in the fold
Truth be told these bars tend to come off the dome
Then carving out like sculptures any inapt idioms
Untoward, but all aboard as we negotiate to shores
Rhythmically dissecting lines from notes down to the chords
Spurting out with purpose, each shoulder touched by swords
Reverse the inertia, pressure gauges scream like condors

Plans (From The Infinity Files)

Hypervigilant for a reason
My kind's in season
A pirate on the highest seas
Heisting, evading high treason

Back at the main cabin, planning on fasting
Stacking bars in a frantic fashion
Pass the cattail, call me Captain
Hoist the sails, make advancements

Off the rails, no caption
Last of the holy grails, no duplication happenin'
Faster than the falling stars or revolving planets
Master of my ship, grip the microphone outstanding

Chaptered, but outlasting lyrics when they're running rampant
Gather in the temple where the best of best's examined
Cruising through the samples, scratches, cadences landed
Like lunar surfaces conducting tides til we're stranded

Real (From The Infinity Files)

I need a pencil sharpener
Uppin' my pen game
Felt tip, wax on Maker's Mark
Paint by numbers - close range

Boundary crossing like stalkers
A bit deranged
Bob Barker parting at 99
...Well played

Darker just before the crack of dawn
Harbinger of Light, passin' through your lawn
Farther from the rookies' realm crisscrossing 'round pawns
Harder when I took myself most seriously in song

Pouring through the blasted doors of sonic corridors
Soaring over mastadons and sabres, prehistoric tours
My fortress is a sand castle, build me far from shore
Of course the course is shorter when we order less is more

Slippin (From The Infinity Files)

A trophy to the host with the most consistent growth
A nod to the technician mixing rhythms coast to coast
A crown of heather woven together, white and rose
The sound of music tokens offers thoughts for your ghost

Dose dependent, staying independent and verbose
Grandiose ambassadors of rap apropos
Honing in on moments ornamented with the glow
Zone in on atonements, we are now in the know

Let's go on a journey, the search continues certainly
To and fro so fervidly until each head has heard of me
Murkin beats and lacing measures so assuredly
Lurking beneath grace and grit and done so coherently

Apparently cohesion of the teamwork reigns intact
Barely breathing but I'm back with a mate from hip hop's past
Carefully creating living legacies and pacts
Damnit we're determined, it's an unforsaken fact!

Killer (From The Infinity Files)

It's a territorial hope affair
Building futures in ancient lairs
Til there's silver in our hair, and fine lines to bear
The guild is thine, watch us work in pairs

Working in volumes, making time stand in columns
Phonograph static encapsulates molecules
Vibrating on the tables like water droplets, now this is possible
Mr and Mrs Illogical

Beats and bars for days, barricades bend and break cuz we're unstoppable
The topics are lethal, beseeching regents and regals
Embodying the Harpy Celaeno, screech like an eagle
Field goals, LB going killer on the beat tho

Meat roasts on the pole above the glowing embers smoke
The infinite encampment, artistry I'll put my stamp in and won't choke

Rip rock, roll and spoke
You can still smell the hope
Folks, every bar is built in shadows of cloaks

Breath control fans the flames highlighting pen strokes
This is the magic of the music- watch as we invoke
Connections so relentless, tightrope walk to the scope
LP, LB, Wilk and Amol- let's go!

Who Is Lady Poetic?

(as featured on The Lady Poetic Mixtape Vol. 1)

I've been listening to hip hop most of my life, at least from a young age
If I had to narrow down a number, I must have been about 8
Started collecting cassette tapes, from all the greats
Outkast, Masta Ace, Spice 1, MC Eiht
When I was 13, I learned how to freestyle
Started practicing my flows, and did this for awhile
Living rooms, basements, driveways, detention
Solo, with family, session after session
When I was 15, at the circle, sitting on the stoop
I wrote my first rap song, then who knew?
That would set into motion, years of writing and rapping
Listening to and appreciating every hip hop facet
Without listening to Canibus, I wouldn't be who I am
Respect to the greatest lyricist to grace the microphone stand

At 22 years old, I recorded my first EP

And solidified my Moniker as LP
From Lyrical Princess to Lady Poetic
I've been reppin' this name for 20 years, feels genetic
Shortly after the EP, I moved around the globe
Learning about medicine, biochemistry, microbes
Did gigs at local shows, multicultural events
Stayed in touch with my music fam wherever I went
Performing and recording when I could
Meeting other artists and producers who would
Have similar interests and tastes in the underground
Mixtape after mixtape, collaborations abound
Forums, journeys of the mind, interactions
That would forever shape my taste, motivations and action
We got deep into the music, the culture, the religion
We stayed immersed in beats and booths, we lived in the kitchen

Then I took a hiatus from laying down tracks
Focused on my career, but never steered off path
From the world which birthed an unbelievable thirst
For creativity, from mainstream to the berth
Of independent artistry, a society in fact

"Hip hop is who we are, and what we do is rap"
We kept up with concerts, and our favorite emcees
Make sure to cop the next drop, whether CD or mp3
After several chapters, a shift in balance at last
I started online open mics, with a friend from hip-hop's past
It re-spawned within me a passion for my craft
And with XPreNN's beats I started working on new drafts
Brushed off my equipment and took the mic in hand
"Hello my old friend", just wait at what we've planned

A resurgence in the community, and now I'm right where I outta be
Released in 2023 my own published book of hip-hop poetry
Panel member on the hip hop podcast Temple of Bars
Recording new songs, reaching for the stars
Dropping lyric videos, working on new hooks
Making plans for the next 50 years of the greatest genre in the books
Be on the lookout for new videos and songs
My heart's in the right place, how can I go wrong?
30 years strong, I've been here all along

Now that you've heard of me, come with me on a journey lifelong
That, y'all, is a snapshot, of the creation of Lady P
I do this for the love, of hip hop, rap, and poetry.
Peace.
Lady Poetic
2024
Hip-hop, hip-hop, hip-hop

Roll Out the Red Carpet

(as featured on the Lady Poetic Mixtape Vol. 1)

A thousand times before, The Apocalypse, The Score
But listen when I twist together different ways to witness more
Parietal lobes light up, highlighting the chorus
Neurons on the line, fire like an orchestra in focus
Grand marquis, short circuit wiring
Amplified in twilight light: Lady P
Roll out the red carpet, hold open the door
Storm's a comin', watch how the lyrics pour
Velvet ropes woven round the curtains, skylines glowing
Lights dim, lime-lights beam, smoke is blowing
Mic check, finger tap, lick lips, shoulders back
Your heart rates now in tune with the bass in the room- how's that?
Tappin' on this laminate and you ain't even clapped
This ones' for the vets, die-hards, and better yet
The one way in the back, the one I haven't met
The ones that's been keeping all of hip hop in check

Systolically the pressure's like the pail moon- rising
Symbolically the weather might impale like lighting
Diabolically I'm feeling selfish, realizing
I'll pray to Christ, not blasphemize, it's my king
Striking symbols, light be nimble, rhyme or riddle?
Sliding toward the middle, the lux is like a triple
Shock ya through ya chakras, enough to make a cripple
Top it off with hotter bars, sweat starts to trickle
Fickle when it comes to timing, talk is tantalizing
Whittle away boundaries while my bounty's finalizing
Sit and stay awhile, ya pulse is normalizing
Imprint upon my prey, protect from perfect timing
Capture your attention, like it's retinas taking pictures
Implant distant memories, stone cold fixtures
Sandy beaches, sidelines, modern mixtures
Shuffle in your seat, wonder what's this new elixir?

From jars of hearts to flies, make no compromise
We alter waves of sine, take integrals to the lines
Fifty yards to start, forsaking passes and fines
A martyr takes one for the team, the tempo's in its prime
Chime in, I'm rhyming like it's 1999

Not likely what you'd like to see, it's one of a kind
Furious like dueling cellos, bending the mind
Swinging pendulums, egg white, colorblind
Coffee black, penny tips, shaky grip, slow to slip
Flippin' out like Money Mike- the ultimate pimp
Spittin bout the ties that bind, you bump in the whip
And nod your head and feel instead each word where you sit
Split screens, wigs, P's and Q's
Pleasing to the ears and not polluting the views
Preceding every starving artist, hardest to choose
Applauding for the LP and I thought you'd approve

Castles Rising

(as featured on The Lady Poetic Mixtape Vol. 1)

This is Wisconsin. This is Michigan
Castles rising. Let us begin
Hip-hop is a castle, major players in the turrets
Banners of the best, waving in the mist-concerted
Winds whipping violently, the symphonic asserted
I've been in the catacombs, but creeping up, make sure you heard it
House established plaques start to chip, but we preserve it
Cursive writtens bound in leather, stacked, predicting verdicts
Dripping candlesticks emit a glow for the deserted
Traversing greystone pillars, float through moats till we've alerted
Grit and blood beneath our nails, a sigil that we've earned it
Emblematic tactics, catapult us towards the surface
Galvanize the drive to raise the bar before we burn it
Moonless skies are crystallized, the motif, we prefer it
Raise the drawbridge, pay the homage, plan to observe it
Whether we collude or battle, every verse is worth it

Horns are blaring in the distant valleys, soul exerted
Mourning's over, unsung heroes vow to return it

Castles rising, you won't see us fall
Perhaps surprising, an undying one for all
Building up an empire, tearing down a fortress
Wielding words of fire, wearing crowns in portraits

Castles rising, you won't see us fall
Perhaps surprising, an undying one for all
Building up an empire, tearing down a fortress
Wielding words of fire, wearing crowns in portraits

Vestiges collected and this message is relayed
Brow beaten, not defeated, scream intentions with rage
Percentages protect us as we go against the grade
Monuments were melted, priceless portraits start to fade
We cyphered in the bailey, back and forth, on bended knee, we prayed
The closet in the keep, boasted garments of crusades
Cloaked in hope and expertise to breach the blockade
Takin and then making names, we charged the light brigade

Casing gates, chasing fame, declined the masquerade
Traipsing up the staircases, our entrances forbade
Spiraling up the taluses, embattlements betrayed
Taking shots through arrow slits, we managed to evade
Premeditate advancement, still so callous on the raid
Fathoming a victory while history is being made
Curtain wall collapses, sunrise turns to shade
Lay down armor set in stone, L.P. and Connor on parade

Castles rising, you won't see us fall
Perhaps surprising, an undying one for all
Building up an empire, tearing down a fortress
Wielding words of fire, wearing crowns of portraits

Wanna Leave

(as featured on the Lady Poetic Mixtape Vol. 1)

Where were you
And where did you go?
When I wanna leave
Didn't you know?

Bad seeds, black sheep, bad blood runs deep
Mad peeps, fact sheets, sad but sons creep
Mom weeps, pop screams, cuz on the streets
One week, stop beef, Unc speaks,
Got a sister off the bottle, one can't put it down
One brother: role model, one on a countdown
Cousin got a new bracelet, on his ankle, on papers
Creepin' on a come up, rocking diamond watch faces
Face it, I'm just saying, it makes more sense to slay it
Prayed on it already, back and forth just pacing
Contemplating next moves- ain't this entertaining?
In the words of MC Lyte I'm "through with the waiting!"

On a plane, on a train, by any means, to keep sane

Without fame, and an unknown name
No more blame, march of dimes down candy lane
Across the ocean, eyes swollen, caustic pain
Swimming solo, dippin dolo, misty rain
Hits my forehead, tread toward the main
Family's functionality or lack there of near left me strained
I pause and I cannot forget, it's all the same
Thicker than water, make me red
Read every book, and still I said
Searched every legend, make my bed
Worked through every kink and not a word was said
Wade through rivers chest deep,
Just to break away and sleep
My soul, My God, I pray to keep
Still waters run deep
Shoulders heave, it's hard to breathe
YOU KNOW what you gotta do, and when to leave

The Rhyme Circle

(as featured on the Lady Poetic Mixtape Vol. 1)

Ah yes, an XPreNN production
Lady Poetic present The Rhyme Circle:

If you wondered for a split second where I was,
This one's for you, and I do this because
It's all for the love
The medicine wheel spins round,
The balancing act has been profound
All along I've been residing in the underground
Lost and found, lock and key
XPreNN and LP
Pairing once again together in perfect harmony
Informing you we never do this marginally
Rather than forcibly, we do this cordially
Engage every cell in your auditory
Bring together a real rap symphony
From the best of beats and a real emcee
Lacing lyrics so intricately
Turn this up a notch if you feeling me

As I ignite your brain chemistry
It was always purposefully
Thank your dopamine and serotonin for me
Whether igneous or metamorphic
This one rocks, bypass the chorus
More porous than litmus when it gorges
On acid, fantastic,
Swim through lakes, from Lochness to Placid
Faltered on fault lines before but just for a fraction
Shout out to the ones bobbin' heads to this madness
I'm in cycle with moon, forgive my candidness
I'm in circle with medicine wheels, never planned this
Bearing fruits like it's Elaeagnus
Offer the best, otherwise hip hop won't stand for this

From the cycle of the moon
To the one beside you
To the rotation of the earth
From the bitter end, to the biggest first
Our verbal execution moves us through hurdles
We work in cycles, stories and circles

Splitting atoms, spitting tongues
Breath control from damaged lungs
Better yet cuz I've just begun
Salute the flute, here come the drums
Come full circle, once undone
Work in circles, what becomes
Of a tireless heart and undying love
Stepping out from under thumbs
Flexing now, amassing heat
Boluses of bars where synapses meet
Street smarts and finer arts do greet
A long courtship of potpourri
Peppered with clever letters
And accolades for jesters
Spades and bones for good measure
Keep it city in windy weather
Even the strongest ties sever
Endeavor after endeavor
It's been my pleasure
Now whether we top the charts, or stay in the dungeon
I'll be bumpin' 5 o clock, and Curmudeon
Brick and mortar build something

Been in my blood even when it wasn't
Red blood cells cycle every four months
Rhymes circles come around once
Medicine wheels make cycles out front
I left out the fillers and mumbling stunts
For circles and cycles, I never planned this
Offer the best or hip hop will never stand for this

From the cycle of the moon
To the one beside you
To the rotation of the earth
From the bitter end, to the biggest first
Our verbal execution moves us through hurdles
We work in cycles, stories and circles

Apex (To the Top!)

(as featured on the Lady Poetic Mixtape Vol. 1)

With secular sophistication the attitudes flow
Poetic in fact but noetic from the go
Stoic in this moment but I thought you should know
We still doctor up the illest lyrics on the microphone

We grew tepedum lucidum to see you in secret
Mic masters on the track, matter fact you can keep it
Bleeping out conundrums, enunciate son
I'm on some elliptical, cryptic-type runs

Sharper than cargo pants or fangs of fer de lance
Viper striking, set you on the seat of your pants
Balance the stance, crane kicks, wipe you on the mat
Politically incorrect and fat chance of that

Preferably the plan will be well executed
With results not having us stranded or clueless
Word plays for days, range from mild to ruthless
I'll body the bars, leaving all remnants useless

Once upon a time we made our way to the apex
Sunsets gone, rhymes fade, pay our respects
Where you going?
To the top!

Stimulating brain waves, convex, concave
This beat is hitting harder than K at a rave
Simulating bravery like there's someone to save
Pulsating widths whip your will to enslave

Battle the best of them, I'm not impressed yet
Reppin' since the 90s and growing with the vets
Plannin' this out, not knowing the rest
Lacing beats with Anno D and puffin my chest

Platooning through lagoons of music, getting stupid
Looping legendary layers, looking like who did it
Scooping sedentary capers, working on who moves it
Fluting futuristic fundamentals, nothing's excluded

Gliding like gazelles against the grain, then unfolding
Winding down like starlings, diamond hands holding

Finding out what sells then start breaking the molding
Timing all will tell, engage in what we'd be holding

Once upon a time we made our way to the apex
Sunsets gone, rhymes fade, pay our respects
Where you going?
To the top!

References and diagnostics, sensei's bowing- you we got this
Prowling through the concrete jungles, watch my prowess
Eyes are glowing, sizing up the prizes, I'm just being honest
Seismic slowing, going where the competition's monstrous

Absconding with the realest hip hops heads across the continent
Wild west out here, we winding up as Most Wanted
Poster child for poetry, no it's not approximate
Possibly I waited just to drop this when I was this confident

Urban Chronicles Cypher (LP's Lyrics)
(as featured on The Lady Poetic Mixtape Vol. 1)

You have now reached the Urban Chronicles cypher,
So I had to get my boys on the track
From '07 to '24, we go way back
We meet once again in the middle
Like the center of an infinity symbol

Once again in future tense they'll call us urban legends
Massive social influences, spread like damage
Caste systems casting doubts upon the average
Unlawfully live, then broadcast it- now that's savage
Imagine the transparent leading up to the scandals
Riots, vandalism- more than we can gamble
Flying off the handle, electricity in ampules
Landing strip, metrics measured international
From New York to the Port, Midwest and up North
Freestyle the verses to toggle back and forth
Ping ponging the signals then playing Contra Force
Outdated reference? Par for the course!
It's idiomatic and we offer no remorse

We don't pass it down, we pass each other the torch
Tearing this apart, melt it down and reforge
Concealing is ironical so drop it on the porch
Revealing measures of the chronicle, not so simple
When pressure is on to slaughter every syllable
Titrating this preparation to the pinnacle
Before you thank me, pause, 'cause my time is billable
Financial disparagement is criminal
But listen when they tell you that it's meant to be livable
Waging wars on everything but what we make is minimal
You wanna relate? I set this one on principal
Pin it between cynical, indifferent or optimistic,
Blossoming business, artistic linquists
Unlikely friendship like ours- so sophistic
Wilkshake runs this up a notch- that why he's been enlisted
One for the road by consistently spinning it
Paycheck to paycheck or minute by minute
Even if it's been one I'll be ready on the mic to spit it
Then set the next verse up for my boy Dermz to rip it!

We meet once again in the middle
Like the center of an infinity symbol

Weaving together stories of urban chronicles
Nothing less than phenomenal

From CC to TOB
Kickin' rhymes since our prime, going on 20 years deep
Weaving together stories of urban chronicles
Nothing less than phenomenal

Overture of the Shrink

(as featured on The Lady Poetic Mixtape Vol. 1)

It's the overture of the shrink
Time to make you think
The future shock has left us on the brink
Panic stricken, missin' minutes within a blink
Neurochemical transmission of writtens now insync
Supplementing strategies with thiamine and zinc
From paper charts to EMRs we chose to uplink
Thorazine to TMS, Rorschach blots to pink
Capsules, pills, injectibles, dissolving in your favorite drink
De-institutionalization, goodbye asylums
Soaring with psychoses linked to Huntington's or prions
Hysterical, empirical evidence to try on
Agitation, mane's are thrashing back and forth like lions
Minds and compounds breaking down, tears into ions
Lobotomize, so in disguise, more simpletons than Simon
Orderlies with badges, hardened shoulders to cry on
Folstein mini mentals, now I'm marching to Zion

Break apart the thoughts, the ones that do you wrong

Elevate your mind and find the rhythm to the beat of your own song
Break apart the thoughts, the ones that do you wrong
Elevate your mind and find the rhythm to the beat of your own song

Like Freud exploiting Jung, I'm imploring different methods
The void has only sprung with migs of misery imbedded
Like Troy to Helen, hell is evidently indebted
Toying with triumphs, Ross' grief is vetted
Tau tangles, different angles, webs netted
State hospitals closing, the families' fretted
Insurance imposes now, insanity is tested
Furiously exposing how the rhapsody rejected
Lunacy Acts passed in periods of madness
Treatise of Madness reads with infinite sadness
Smashing through the ceiling when the thoughts go back to blackness
Passing through the Anatomy of Melancholy like an atlas
At last restraints yanked around the limbs like a tunica
Cast complaints, don't wait for what disorders'll do to ya

Healers are trying to help, not meant to ruin ya
Let's set this one up for success or send em back to Utica

Break apart the thoughts, the ones that do you wrong
Elevate your mind and find the rhythm to the beat of your own song
Break apart the thoughts, the ones that do you wrong
Elevate your mind and find the rhythm to the beat of your own song

Phrenology, leather couches, trials and articles
Psychology never vouches for vials filled with particles
Possibly moving mountains, tired but honorable
Confiscating left brain/right brain traffic- remarkable
Limited in tools, arts and science in the arsenal
Ridiculed, the heart and mind dance like a carnival
Abused, tied the noose, advancements arbitral
See you is 6 months, schedule hierarchical
The looking glass was cracked, the glass menegerie intact
The elephant in the room, forced us to react
Taboo treatments reaching for a course to enact
Rendezvous in secret, not a glorified act

Substance use skews results, dramatic impact
Get past misconceptions, rails realign on track
Prescription pads collecting dust, activities stacked
Look for glimmers, bury triggers, be matter of fact

Break apart the thoughts, the ones that do you wrong
Elevate your mind and find the rhythm to the beat of your
own song
Break apart the thoughts, the ones that do you wrong
Elevate your mind and find the rhythm to the beat of your
own song

Wavelength

(as featured on The Lady Poetic Mixtape Vol. 1)

Oceans apart and minutes between
The token to start and finish the scene
Once spoken apart, now it seems
The focus is sharp, and legacy supreme

The wavelengths are steady, hungry emcees ready
Victoria Lake to Serengeti
Peaks to valleys, peace of plenty
Twenty odd years, come and get me
Navigating landscape changes
Gravitating making plans for stages
Releasing birds from cages
From mind and heart to pen and pages
Winning wars and pinning wages
You couldn't tame us
These are from the days when I was bumpin' Almost
Famous (ha)
Look at us- off to the races
Let's face it- years built up to make this

Creating moves on modern pavements
Sometimes I suffocate with anticipation
But as quickly as my blood is pumping I'm still aiming
Hope you feel me when I'm saying
There's no shame in trying to make it
Get at me on this wavelength and let's elevate it
The energy is off the chain, reactivate it
The synergistic, rhythmic type, split the tape deck!

Oceans apart and minutes between
The token to start and finish the scene
Once spoken apart, now it seems
The focus is sharp, and legacy supreme

The Harpy Celaeno 2025

(Updated as for the Storyteller's Page EP)

Introduce King Phineus, with a gift of prophecy from Zeus
Blinded, driven to the island, starved and marked as obtuse
Swarming in the storm winds, enter in the harpies
Snatching, grabbing, leave you stranded, robbing all catharsis

This hell perpetuated 'til the Argonaut's arrival
Phineus promised guidance, if aided in survival
They perished by the hands of the Boreads from the North Wind
They fled and fell, few were spared, much to his chagrin

One harpy fell to the Tigris, the other reached Echinades
These haggard beasts, claws and teeth, birds of a feather, face of a lady
Freed by Iris and Hermes, Phineus' fate was promised
He then guided the Argonauts with little to admonish

Monstrous and beyond us, daughters of Thaumus

The Harpy Calaeno, beast of burden, honored construct
Mommy Fortuna held her, if you appreciate the reference
Outlined by ancient oracles, foretold a polished preference

Dwell in darkness, birds of a feather
We meld in sharpness, bring words together
Stark raving madness, it's mystical
A relic waiting, in the abyss for you

The hounds of mighty Zeus, the ministers of thunder
Vicious, cruel and violent, masters of the plunder
Residing in the caves of Crete or islands of Strophades
Guardians of the underworld, give a nod to Hades

Circle back to the seventh ring of hell, note Dante
Allighieri
Who pens the tales of these morphous females, no ordinary
Crying lamentations through the tortured, twisted trees
Uttering prophecies as it seems and brings you to your
knees

The Trojans fled in fear at hearing the omen from Celaeno
The progeny of Electra, with Ocythoe and Aello
Agents of abduction- if you disappear from Earth
Carried to Tartarus, silenced and stripped of worth

Hateful drops drip from their eyes, creatures of repulsion
Bestowing onto you fatal famine like compulsion
Save one, the Dark One, Celaeno freed by The Last
Held captive, how exceptional, future bleeds into the past

Dwell in darkness, birds of a feather
We meld in sharpness, bring words together
Stark raving madness, it's mystical
A relic waiting, in the abyss for you

Escort the scorned to blessed fields
For those who mourned the message sealed
The woes torn at angelic heels
Disclosures forged in melted steel

Fiercest winds she did embody
Piercing sins, resist so calmly
Cursing myths insisting oddly
Birthing seven stars as godly

Hidden from Orion, traced as constellations
Extinguished in the ninth labor without hesitation
Written as the signs above the gates of creation
Sinister, divine, plucking harp strings with patience

Fading from the culture's breath, glance from the side
Lay me on the vultures breast, enhance my demise
Draining colors from the nest, dance in the night
Gravely, alchemist of death, cast out the light

Locate her in Cthulhu (Khlul-hloo) Mythos, end with a sigh
Funerary priestess, present when end is nigh
Luminary beast, prophetic talents arise
She turned to me and said, "We are sisters, you and I"

The Fall of Maximilien Robespierre (Coup d'état of 9 Thermidor)

(as featured on the Storyteller's Page EP)

France, Paris 1793

Du règne de la terreur, supervisé
À la scène mouvementée de la guillotine

Bloodthirsty deviate, timid bourgeois?
Persecuted patriot, once deputy of Artois
Undone mercy, point to pivot from applaud
Surely prudent to revisit: 9 Thermidor, Coup d'etat

Leader of the Jacobins
Speaker in these moments
Seeker of eminence, resist dethronement
Feature the facts, Preach to the loyalists

Young Maximillien, born in Arras
Unsung recipient, learned philosophy and law
Louis le Grand constituents, first lawyer then judge

Once among respected, now bearing their grudge

Defending the indigent, he would protest
Condemning injustice, so distinguished
Politically propelled until it lead to his death
Ultimately compelled by The Law of Suspects

Supremely confident with umpteen accomplishments
Committee of Public Safety, ultimately dominant
Teetering on the pendulum, seesawing with parliament
Cheering from speeches, the king's actions despotic

Louis the 16th, crown gripped and teeth gnashed
Would he abolish the monarchy, slip past the greed's math
Guilty of treason, found, Robespierre did advocate
With rhyme or reason, now, it's 'off with his head'

Bloodthirsty deviate, timid bourgeois?
Persecuted patriot, once deputy of Artois
Undone mercy, point to pivot from applaud
Surely prudent to revisit: 9 Thermidor, Coup d'etat

Invade the Convention, the spark that lit the Terror
The debate of well-intention, hit the mark in error
To create a liberation, when it's dark and wishes bear
The indefatigable Maximillien, departs as his own heir

A virtuous republic, an unyielding quest
The merciless subjugate, concealing powers to cement
Purposeful savagery, stealing hours to repent
Worse, still, the enemies cowered at the threats

Inflation ran rampant, embittered by slander,
tyrannical plans in hand withered within a manner
When the National Convention delivered the end of his chapter
The program dismantled, on whispered propaganda

Legislations, broken bread, burgundy at feet
Revolution, spoken urgently in the streets
Pen and pages to orations, unemployment peaked
Solutions opened fervently, conspirator's deceit

Royals grew in lavish wealth, commoners would plead

Spoils strewn, habits of health, admonishers would siege
Turmoil soon at his arrest, camaraderie, a liege
Glorified, villainized...dome decree

Bloodthirsty deviate, timid bourgeois?
Persecuted patriot, once deputy of Artois
Undone mercy, point to pivot from applaud
Surely prudent to revisit: 9 Thermidor, Coup d'etat

Fight the common enemy with only sword of law
Ignite the solemn remedies, Hotel de Ville, broken jaw
Despite the nods or friendlies, he potentiates the flaw
Heighten the sonic energies, open the ports of call

Imprisonment refused at Luxembourg by the warden
Innocent unless recused, once the word had warned him
An instant finish was imbued, a gun was awarded
Ambiguous if self inflicted, or done by soldiers

An outlaw now declared, and as fate would have it
On 9 Thermidor, he was arrested and branded
Bandaged and battered, an outlandish capture

Fanatical tyrant with wit, class and banter

Flamboyant enacter, descending from power
Enjoyments to factor, upending suns over towers
From voices of lecture, a reign turning sour
Your choice how to measure, an unending hour

Bloodthirsty deviate, timid bourgeois?
Persecuted patriot, once deputy of Artois
Undone mercy, point to pivot from applaud
Surely prudent to revisit: 9 Thermidor, Coup d'etat

The screaming was primal, the execution swift
The meaning is mindful, the truth lies in rifts
Being insightful, duty rises and shifts
Seemingly prideful, Preach to the loyalists

((From the Reign of Terror, overseen
To the turbulent scene at the guillotine))

The Fall of Maximillien Robespierre
la fin

"Save Him"

(as featured on the Storyteller's Page EP)

"9-1-1, what's your emergency?"

A middle aged reporter just collapsed
Blood's trickling down his face, he fell backwards from the blast
His airways clear, I compressed his chest
Then he exsanguinated from the gash beneath his vest
Applying pressure to the wound, send someone for Town Hall!

"Paramedics are en route, thank you for your call."

I must have missed it, but when we enlisted, our vision was explicit
Why risk it for this band of invalids, take a glimpse, kid-
Criminalistics. position hidden, protect all footage, save children and women
Now you're slippin' on logistics, the requisite exodus
Exit left, the less amiss is all of this as we slip through the

mist
Be swift and signal the syndicate, do insist
Wipe the prints, ignite the risk, I'll bring the journalist
Quick to flip the script and insert a twist.
With the exception of any questions, you are dismissed.

Beg your pardon but aside from the jargon we caused him harm
and Sargeant, we can ring the alarm and
Abort the course and transport this man to a hospital
Resorting to force, or the recourse cannot be possible

An obstacle, yes, but not worth jeopardizing
A probable solution brews forth on the horizon
A methodical physician with resistance & finesse
No insurance, no fuzz, no questions asked

What are we waiting for?
Let's go
Gather the gear, take it slow

"No indemnification, no nonsense, capisce?

No identification, no confidence breech
Describe the situation, he's unstable, no lies
I'll revive him on the table and get my supplies
Bradycardic, blood loss and contusions
Lethargic, grab the cart and exhaust any transfusions
18 gauge, lidocaine, call a time out
Nylon 5-0 black sutures for when he bleeds out
Forceps and scalpel, and no guarantees
Consort by the mantle, leave it to me, please"

Save him
Why didn't you save him?

You only saved yourself

Crimson gauze piled high
Wisdom flawed, laid beside,
Exasperated, heard her sigh
Weak and jaded, murmuring "I tried"
It was a slight when you arrived,
He was on the line with the longest kiss goodnight
She wiped her brow, somehow I thought I saw her cry

Despite the vows, now the water's running dry
Integrity was compromised, though, had he survived
I raised my eyes and thought it wise so not to imply

“Please gather the remains and be on your way
You'd rather not be seen around these parts this time of day”

“We thank you for your efforts, and we're finding a way”
Defeated ranks dismembered past the operating bay

The forecast was foreboding
I held back my emotions, choking
Which way are we going?
Philosophically, unknowing
Pin back hope to say it's growing
Blinded by the lines blurred and burdens towing
My cowardice is owning
My disbelief is showing

Rapidly, revengefully, replayed the days events
Heavily, mentally, maybe making sense

We'd all have our regrets
I found myself replaying mine repeatedly inside my head
I'd say to her, “save him. Why didn't you save him?”

Ode to the One From the Prophecy

(as featured on the Storyteller's Page EP)

Ay... Ay.. Ok..
This is beautiful, LB. This is a whole vibe.
It's an ode.

An ode to mi familia
So glad to meet ya
I know it's been a few seasons
But now I'm here to greet ya
You know I'm introverted
I live inside my head til I spill out the words
Then my tongue is twisting, twirling
Stumbling, but I'm still learning
You feel me when I'm hurting
You're curious when I'm searching
My absence senses a burden
Forgive the esotericism
And lack of focus when the wheels are turning
What we have: eternal, the flame burning
No matter how it's worded,

I give my life to you on purpose
It's more than time that you heard this:

I'd be wading
But never for you
Breath was bated
And then you came through

When I found out you were arriving
Fear spread through my body
And I'm not gonna lie, a tiny part of me
was excited for you, bunny
My body changed and I was scared
Didn't feel fully prepared
Hold me up on this one y'all,
While my soul is bared
You came into this world
Mi angel, mi hija, my darling little girl
This is my bond, this is my word
Your first laugh was the greatest sound I ever heard
That's not to say you don't have a way of making me
nervous

From your first cry, and when I first laid eyes, you were perfect
I couldn't know for sure, for certain
Til I peered behind the curtain
I give my life to you on purpose
Just a few short years into it
And I'm already overdue for this
It's more than time that you heard this:

I'll be wading
But never for you
Breath was bated
And then you came through

Here's to the ones, who try to hold me up
My partners in life, puttin' up with my stuff
Whether ultra energetic, or slightly neurotic
Paralyzed with anxiety, or acting obnoxious
Looking at stars, planning plane trips to planets
Driving fast cars, turning projects to mansions
Lyfe happens, and some circumstances? can't stand it
The lone wolf with a pack, that's how we gone plan it

Ya growin' on me now, kid, mama bear mode if demanded
Sobering and focused, on the fritz and frantic
Te amo princesita, even when you're reprimanded
It's the little things- you're tiny hand inside of my hand and
The silly things, the spirit of the room- you command it
I'll miss these days and pray I never take you for granted
Sheer brilliance, from your mind to your eyes, and your
smile
This is long overdue- 'case you ain't heard it in awhile:

I'll be wading
But never for you
Breath was bated
And then you came through

Ay ay

To Antigua, With Love
(as featured on the Storyteller's Page EP)

I will remember you forever
Even if
Even if

Even if your turquoise waters weren't the richest that I'd seen
And the sun hadn't kissed then burnt my skin
Even if it was a dream
I 'll remember you forever
You oughta know what I mean
I miss your ocean's mist
The chances I missed
True love, loss and bliss
Even if
Even if

Now's the time, I take to give to you
The homage you deserve for everything you put me through

You woke me up, from my core, to my view
You broke my heart, so I left a piece for you
It's on the sand near Blue Waters
Just past the palm trees
Not far from the true shore
Take a left near Crosbies
Then head down to Sand Piper,
Where lingers traces of my soul
The diving birds and speechless words
White sands, I was whole
Fuschia flowers, colors bold
Beautiful hours, never told
Even the hottest nights could sometimes get cold
Even the strongest hands could fold
Even the strongest outer shells could mold
Even if
Even if

Even if your turquoise waters weren't the richest that I'd seen
And the sun hadn't kissed then burnt my skin
Even if it was a dream

I 'll remember you forever
You oughta know what I mean
I miss your ocean's mist
The chances I missed
True love, loss and bliss
Even if

Even if I hadn't left you
I promise I'd never regret you
Your stars were brilliant, by the millions
Sparkling at me like you meant to
The crickets chirping words of wisdom in a rhythmic tune
Like a midnight orchestra of nature
In your arms I couldn't feel safer
You made me braver
You made me major
Even if I didn't know it then
You helped to save her
A favor for a favor
Didn't you know you've be with me every day
and never been a stranger?
Even in times of danger

Performances, examinations
Man you were a game changer
Even if
Even if

Even if your turquoise waters weren't the richest that I'd seen
And the sun hadn't kissed then burnt my skin
Even if it was a dream
I 'll remember you forever
You oughta know what I mean
I miss your ocean's mist
The chances I missed
True love, loss and bliss
Even if
Even if

Even if I could see you right now
I don't know what I'd do
I don't know how
I imagine myself steppin' off the plane
Wait through hours to go through customs

Just to see your face again
I'd drive past Sticky Wicket
And head for the ocean
Where the rhythm of the tides at the same pace as my heart beat's motion
I'd find you ever where I missed you
Even if some things had changed
This love would never do without you
Even if I never see you again, or not for long
I feel you when my eyes glisten
When I replay our song
Even if you stay a memory
To Antigua, With Love,
Love always,
LP

Even if your turquoise waters weren't the richest that I'd seen
And the sun hadn't kissed then burnt my skin
Even if it was a dream
I 'll remember you forever
You oughta know what I mean

I miss your ocean's mist
The chances I missed
True love, loss and bliss
Even if
Even if

I will remember you forever
Even if

Square Roots!

(as featured on the Storyteller's Page EP)

Yo- I know you didn't think every song on this album was gonna be all sweet and poetic, pretty and shit..
We still get gully 'round here
Chea
Square Roots!

We've been on a mission to listen to the sickest lyrics in existence
We'll persist until it's finished
Pull up a chair, I can see you in the distance
Furlough the stares, we don't feed into resistance
The most musically prepared conglomerate of misfits
Toast to the rare, and the need to be consistent
No need to boast or bare, read between the writtens
Ferocious and fair, the beat's got me smitten

Mercenaries Battle Cry
Picture This- Do or Die
Ghetto Dope

Aquemini
Rip the Jacker
Please Don't Cry
Lyte as a Rock
The World is Mind
Illmatic
Still I Rise
Hardcore
Ready to Die

Chea!
(Gully)

Yo, we cut from a different cloth, we celebrate our roots
Give flowers to the vets, we square off in the booth
Chea
Square Roots!

At first I found myself in battle mode then I refocused
The worst was over, and then at last I noticed
Nothing's holding us back, but everything to hold us
Something told us to silence her, or try to choke us

The quest is fully on- a fine prognosis
The best laid it down, time for us to mold it
Be the change you want to see, not change opponents
No stranger than you and me, let's take a moment:

Black Reign
The Diary
Sittin on Chrome
Very Necessary
Soul Survivor
Last of a Dying Breed
It's Dark and Hell is Hot
The Infamy
Things Fall Apart
Bio: Chemistry
Paid in Full
Legal Drug Money
Capital Punishment
6 Feet Deep
Chea!
(Gully)

Yo, Know where you come from, before you get on that mic, when you get on the stage
Lady Poetic: Storyteller's Page
Chea
Square Roots!

The Golden Era raised me, how fortunate was I
Spoke of the majors, a disproportionate rise
Told off conveyors, it's tournament time
The viola players, and organists' rhyme
Heavy Mental, Back for the First Time
Vinyls, cassette tapes in crates and my mind
Finding the new greats, with every bar and line
I'll keep it going- just give me the sign

Like Water For Chocolate
Supa Dupa Fly
Muddy Waters
Black on Both Sides
Only Built for Cuban Lynx
Doggystyle
Madvillainy

Violent by Design

Internal Affairs

Everything's Fine

The Big Picture

Jurassic 5

Chea!

(Gully)

Temple of Bars Quick 16: One

Walking out the front doors of the kingdom
Hip hop music is the motif of this dominion
Been in it for a minute, basically from the beginning
Bar and conscious heavy, I bet you now that's winning

Whimsically my mind's up in the exosphere
I met you here, devising plans for the next year
My commitments keep me centered near
Expectations gravitating, but thankfully it's far from fear

Well aware of the importance of securing future goals
Fairly short notice but once in a moment that's how it goes
Barely definable, dodging, ducking, taking throws
Gutter rats and habitats expelled us so who knows

Constraining, navigating through waters perilous
But I'm a Goddamn pirate compared to the apparentness
Mixtape, full album, podcast, don't be querulous
Double Board certified, one day professor emeritus

Temple of Bars Quick 16: Two

What sort of content matter can I try to exhibit?
Religious, medical, mythological, scientific?
Basic or cryptic? Low key or prolific?
Blunt or sarcastic? Mysterious or misfit?

Easter eggs lined between lines of hieroglyphics
Complexity level- advanced or simplistic?
What type of mood we going for- somber or ecstatic?
What about delivery- choppy or rhythmatic?

Candid or transparent? Approachable or esoteric?
As novice as possible or positing merit?
Talk to me about cadence- fluid or tasteless?
Is the content profound or essentially baseless

Is the wordplay clever, are the doubles adjacent?
What about tone- gritty, smooth or impatient?
Are the layers cohesive, respectful or graceless?
Do we appeal to the novice or aim for the favorites?

The Heart of Hip Hop

The heart of hip hop is truncated, gets ablated
The atriums serve as stadiums and some rhythms are overrated
Electrical readings, spiked and jagged
Internal bleedings leading microphone magnets

Just as joints are punctuated, some intervals get prolongated
QRS complex as lyrics are updated
Pumpin like the bass is thumpin
Beats per minute get it jumpin

Ventricles collecting pools
Queen of the Geeks gets ridiculed
Now ain't that something?
Physiologically getting redundant

The muscles are tough but get friable from
All the overuse like the last speakers you're bumping
A fox for your gun now I'm over here hunting

You live in my chest, I digress, never stunting

Vowels

Illicit instances insist we breed
Infinite instruments with imminent speed
Illustrate irritants irrevocably
Intrinsic implicit instincts succeed

Egregiously emphysemic emcees plead
Effortless energies enter indeed
Eminent embassies exit on steeds
Extricate endlessly every deed

Ominous offerings obstruct the feed
Ornery optimists obfuscate seeds
Opulent oddities opt in the need
Operant olympiads officiate the freed

Auspicious antithesis applauds the creed
Armaments arduously archive the greed
Animalistic ambivalence accepts the lead
Arguably amplifying any and all we read.

eschatological

It was a dark and stormy night, I saw the flicker of the lights
I parked and ordinarily I might bicker bout what's right
Then like a domino effect, the neighborhood once bright
Fell jet black and just like that, in kicked flight or flight
Ejected from my ride as I scrutinize the surrounding site
Infected people walking outside, looking up towards the skies
My eyes were horrified, my mind was seldom surprised
The moment culture glorified just happened in real time
The sounds of the explosions rippled through me to my bones
The town now in corrosion, this one hits close to home
The beating of mi corazon, the buzzing of the flocks of drones
Smells of burning rubber, screamings in a piercing tone
Smoke and flames, ash and metal rain
Helter Skelter, Doomsday- Apocalypse- it's all the same
Solidify your shelter, pray and preach to hold me sane
Fortify for any weather, safe to say for this I trained

This is not a dream. This is not a drill
Electric sheep are stargazing in your horizon,
compromising your will.

This is not a dream. This is not a drill
Electric sheep are stargazing in your horizon,
compromising your will.

Mortified, head to the cellar, gather clothes for all terrain
Torches, maps of indwellers, batteries, matches and butane
Surgical supplies, blankets, candles, swords and chains
Pen and paper for the storyteller, when we wax and wain
Arcane sciences and scriptures could have prepared us
Membranes to the amygdalas inherently scared us
Moving up the foodchain, forced to fight what impairs us
Grooving, start the entrain, source to meet at the terrace
Double check the weaponry, suture kits, plaster of paris
A couple checks for seven seas, fit for an heiress
Ferrous fumes, and blood stained tombs lead us through lairs
Careless planning extricates the wombs of well-intentioned prayers

Soothsayers at mountain peaks await the gates for heaven's stairs
Proof that plain and meek, shall inherit the fates of unaware
Aloof and truth be told, we take our place in common squares
Noose is tightening around the globe, latest state of affairs

This is not a dream. This is not a drill
Electric sheep are stargazing in your horizon, compromising your will.

This is not a dream. This is not a drill
Electric sheep are stargazing in your horizon, compromising your will.

Whiplash, burn and crash, molotovs, machetes slash
Roadrash, learn and match, olive branch, plenty to pass
Hidden stash, discern the catch, rhythms escalating fast
Eschatological, now I'm haunted by my past
Reload the shotty, oil up kitana blades
Exercise our bodies, toil for manana's serenade
Memorize where commodities outline grids and raids

Prophesize when the plans may foil, loyalists dissuade
I'm camouflaged in guts and mud
Bandaged bandits, gaskets thud
Branded mascots, caskets plugged
Sabotage the saviors plans- you promised us this wouldn't
flood
Vagabonds will band together, persist against the rapture
Songs and ballads sadly wish they could capture
Glimmers and the low-lights of a somewhat hopeless
chapter
Dimmer grows the prose- I never guaranteed an ever after...

The Food Wrap

We got raps about cars, money and ice
Lyrics about science & dimes looking nice
Raps about politics, nonsense and moods
What I really want to hear though is a rap about food!
Give me some grits and bacon, sausage and biscuits
Piping hot out the pan, burn my tongue? Yo I'll risk it
Scramble some eggs, add some hash browns and toast
Make them pancakes fat and fluffy,
But what I love the most: waffles and whipped cream, covered in berries
Drizzle the syzurp, coffee creamer- non dairy
That'll start me off right, just in time for a snack
Apples and peanut butter, mackin on that
Celery, raisins, chips of every flavor
Sweet, salty, spicy, so many options to savor
Let's grab some ho-hos and twinkies, maybe a honey bun or two
Cheetos and Fritos, a Take 5 and Mt Dew
Get my belly to settle, cuz ope! Here comes lunch
Deli meat for a sandwich with lettuce for crunch

Soups or salads? Dinner rolls and dressing
It's not all I can eat but I'm not second guessing
I'll challenge this appetite, snag a cold pop
Soufflés and lemonade, it's going over the top
Cherry pie ala mode, burgers with pickles
Cooking up dinner later's bound to be fickle
I'll take a brief hiatus, perhaps sip a ginger ale
Then prep the appetizer, oysters or snail?
Sautéed asparagus, flame-broiled salmon
I'm gorging myself like a last-meal eating madman

"Burgers, tacos, pizza
Shake, shake, shake
How much more gourmet food
can my tummy take?"

Lobster tail please, then bust out the steaks
My A1 since day one? Caramel cake
White chocolate pretzels, Pringles, tilapia
My favorite of all? Pepperoni pizza
Half no cheese, red peppers, thin crust
I'll max the whole pie, this is a must

Yo let's work in some dal, or pindi Chana
Chicken korma, or schwarma then flambéd banana
Lasagna and pasta, angel hair or Al dente
Calzones and neck bones, eating ham on the frenzy
Fire up the grill for some pork chops and brats
French fries, onion rings, tator tots
Hot out the oven, I'm lovin the grub
Now let's whip up some tacos to show my tummy love
Fajitas, sangria, tortillas and dip
Caviar by the bar as I'm wiping my lips
Coconut cream pie, New York cheesecake
Cut me a strip off that T-bone or flank
Pasteles de yucca, pinchos, mufongo
The taste of French crepes on the tip of my tongue though
Macaroons, truffles, yeah I'll hustle for those
Apple pie tarts in the shape of a rose
Ayo we can get fancy, we can get hood
Sushi rolls, pot of greens, damn that sounds good
Doritos for days, chicken soup for the soul
Chili and rye bread? Hook up a bowl
I'm a fool for some cornbread, sweet potato pie
Chitlens I'll pass on, but pass me a thigh

Wing or a breast, deep fried is the best
Douse it in hot sauce then lick up the mess
Popsicles, sundaes, smoothies galore
I'll eat everything twice then save room for more!

"Burgers, tacos, pizza
Shake, shake, shake
How much more gourmet food
Can my tummy take?"

Man I'm just getting started, roll me up a cannoli
Toasted ravioli, fresh guacamole
I'll go nuts for donuts, walnuts, pecans
Cajun turkey topped with a sesame bun
Brownies and custard, tres leche and flan
Broccolini, fettuccine , Alfredo Parmesan
Rib tips, prawns, crab legs, butter drawn
Snickerdoodle cookies and brookies, I'm gone

Baked potatoes, chives, sour cream
Danishes laden with frosting, cream cheese
Fried rice and fish sticks, sourdough bowls

Thick stews, seared tuna smoked over coals
Coco puffs , pizza puffs, flamin hots, Dots
Slushies, hush puppies, Bon bons, garlic knots
Pistachio pie, deviled eggs, turkey legs
Cranberries, pumpkin pie made with nutmeg
Watermelon slices, spices, casseroles
General Taos by the mound, poke bowls
Paninis , empanadas, frittatas and omelets
Fresh pressed juices in glasses and goblets
Potstickers and soy sauce, alligator jerky
Thai iced tea and a coconut Curry
Spaghetti with meatballs, muffins, green beans
Scallops and clam strips, a seafood lovers dream
Lollipops and gobstoppers, jalapeño poppers
Artichoke hearts, red peppers, cauliflower
Makin my mouth water, just smell the aroma
Then start it all over right after my food coma

"Burgers, tacos, pizza
Shake, shake, shake
How much more gourmet food
Can my tummy take?"

Winter Fire (Murdered by Words)

Winter Fire, January Embers
I burn there, too.

Let's build this Winter Fire. One bar at a time.

When the windchill hits below zero, sins populate heroes
Primitive myths will tilt the spherical
Pacing of the solstice, lacing fire with the coldest
Faceless ghosts wrote this, in a crate of stolen moments
Creating pyres from writtens unfolded, once untold to us
Mating sire and sorceress, numb and hopeless
Chases in the mire, sold a panoramic focus
Embrace the heat entire, boasting record lows that broke us
Tip toeing up the summit, wintry mixes run it
Blood flows slow- love it, blisters under thumbs, hunted
Ceremonies funded, whispers in the frozen tundra
Slippin' in the splits of thin ice, now I'm going under
Respiratory rates plummet, face is turning blue
Sanitarium gates rusted, I burn there, too
Magistrates gutted, discerning, bears a clue

Submerged in icy surfaces, time to spark the fuel

Silver flames enraged the sky, crawling on the bank
Filter ways to tame the cries, calling from the lake
Brumal grays encase what dies, stalling frosted breaks
Brutal days before us lie, these are most appalling stakes
Adjacent to the visceral sting, hopeful for spring
It made the most miserable fling, the larks could sing
Vocal cords turned to ice, mid-dusk before the fall of night
It was the most atrocious sight
Now preparing for flights, within perpetual midnights
How daring as we might, spinning conceptual highlights
Frowns and glaring gazes- since been helpful in this plight
Tearing down in blazes, wouldn't tell you when I'm right
Gone til November, moved to a Cold December
Murdered by words grooved to a bolder splendor
Invierno avanza lentamente- remember
Crescendo meant to say, I begged for better weather

Mercury's mark is absent, like the sun ray's enchantment
Work with me in dark, regret the maze's attachment
Search for falling stars collecting pages of ashes

Inferno yields the bars, besting winter's magic
January garnets guarded barren sinner's, tragic
Can you hear me argue, tearin' thinner bits of branches
Planning to disarm you in the midst of brittle trances
Wearing chinks in armor, devastated simple glances
Fancy lunar wilderness whipped past fragile winds
Demanding sooner instances of dripping candle's singe
Planning doom for minutes just to trample on the wings
Taiga's scanned then finished once the falcon starts to sing
Thawing out from friction when the desert's getting warmer
Calling out the kinship when the cinders get to smolder
I'm all in, sweat's drippin', grasping to get older
One day, January embers wither, coulda told her

Spring Challenge (From BhD the DJ's Spring Challenge)

Time to Spring into challenge mode
Amplify every node.

Hope Spring's eternal
Like every lesson unlearned from a higher height and inner circle
Dope instrumental
Bats in the belfry messing with the turn of the tides while winners emerge through
Growth potential
Fire, envy, mentions burn then coincide while the biggest words cue
Float through the avenue
Hell-bent treachery in verses tied up, certainly absurd to you
Goat status, bop ya head to this madness, have at it'

Other worldly, other planet
Uncover the creed under a moonlit magic
The best at bending the bars, to meet my cause, any other

way, wouldn't have it
There's no other contenders- that's how I planned it

Vanish into an unseen vantage, points to the baddest on this time stamp
Candid cameos in Sanskrit, bootlegs dubbed and passed out by chance
Landed in Central Standard, Spring's Equinox was flattered
Ravished in archaic fashion, planted just when the last frost's banished

Kismet advantage
Zealous, frantic, quicker then the wilted seedling reaching for the sun- slanted
Xyris in full bloom- imagine. Dragon Days upon us, gonna cost us one
BhD's Spring Challenge

(Can you find the Easter Egg in the lyrics?)

LP's Lyrics for Bis Posse Cut 2025

Suivez-moi? Since '98- believe it
Three discrete occasions, the greatest to receive it
Indiana to Virginia, out in LA
To the ends of the Earth- it was written this way

The bar's out of reach, so I'll swim there with my feet
The hard charts got bleached, so I read, baring my teeth
Pardon the breech, but we'll get there when we meet
Farther from infinity, nowhere til it's complete

The amplification process of neuronal expedition
I'll be damned if I miss this, mental portals keep on glitching
A Scanner Darkly proposition, the fortitude of the vision
Vanish ever? Hardly- this bond has sworn me to keep spittin'

If the timeline gets skewed, recite the perfect rhyme
Yet when it's devised, improved and publicized
If the mind's eye gets bruised, realign and emphasize

Protect the rhyme and choose us til the meter says "9-9-9-9..."

To the O.C.

Bonds are covalent
Hands tied, ain't it?

I came for the music
But the truth is
I'm swept into music making mayhem
Ruthless

It's the wizard behind the curtain, Dorothy's on stage
From the Mixtape, from the Chambers, to the Storyteller's Page
Craving the notes thrown from Dopamine's rage
Untaming the tasks like a mastermind mage
It's not a cat and mouse tango- we're leopards and jaguars
We're stacking a house, made out of measures, bass and bars
Gotta knack for arousing undead treasures from sandbars
The impact sounding like those go-getters gone too far
There's a crack in my rose colored glasses
A slap cuz we know the endorphin fueled chasms

Kept fracturing most of the novelty gasms
Mastering poise in the face while I fathom
The planned-out encounter, next lifetime? Next hour?
Candid as I scour the progenitive power
Of Chemists, the next lesson plays in the parlor
Did I mention the next question stays on my honor?

Bonds are covalent
Hands tied, ain't it?

I calculated exactly zero seconds to waste
So to spend one with you- I'm defining cachet
Grace me with beats that I bet you I'll lace
Refine my choice, fuck up outta this place
Right now the noise tried to challenge my dignity
Slighted, engrossed by the waves of simplicity
I've been here before in the zenith's epiphany
But never with you, between us it's a symphony
Stick with me, watch us grow, I'll take us places
Respectfully speaking, leaving hands off the faces.
Keep it cerebral people, somatic's off the table
Endearingly though, when we meet between fables

Hear me commend your demeanor and drive
My fall will be silent, fly back to the hive
Speak to me in rhymes, I'll decipher then slide
Right back to the limerence, and bid you goodnight

Bonds are covalent
Hands tied, ain't it?

I came for the music
But the truth is
I'm swept into music making mayhem
Ruthless

To the OC!
I came for the music
But the truth is
I'm swept into music making mayhem
Ruthless.

LP's Verse from Cybernetic
(a Temple Heads Collabo)

I've broken bread with the Gods
There's more to bake, what are the odds?
Grandiose in nature, but mostly in my thoughts
Swam over the Great Barrier Reef for the cause
Stood in front of the Eiffel Tower just to spit bars
Authored the book a Grand Master found impressive
Offered the finest lyrics, Ever After, irrespective
In Sabi Sands mingling with leopards
Looked out of God's Window for perspective
Bowed before Christ the Redeemer, stood at Pearl Harbor
Vowed to save lives, stay true to the Poor Pauper
Fought for her, exhausted her, ran 2 marathons for her
Bore a daughter for her, dusted the MF crown off for her
Absconded with the Temple, penned as awesome song for her
I'd wanna ride along if I was ya
I'd belong to the Temple of Bars if I was ya...

(and I think about the way that things could be
and I hope that one day you and I will see
In my mind's eye, I know that we
are superhuman)

Sand Stones
(an Azimuth Collabo)

I got an all inclusive ridiculously produced hit
Brought to you exclusively from the realest to do it
Painting on canvases words from the scriptures
Making advancements unseen in the pictures

I got a call from the music who insisted I lose it
Fought to reintroduce this prudent fruitfulness
Changing up stanzas in verses with fissures
Framing the master plan rehearsed with distant teachers

This is timeless work, relentless research
This is the result of the cogs in the wheel that searched and hurt
We find sandstones in dirt, pretenses immersed
It culminates past the fog, a beacon pleading at first

A lemniscate in the layers of the infinite trip
A friendship embedded and catered to rip
Into endless melodies mirrored in print

Tendencies to drift are short lived, bring me back to this!

A common thread like silk around snares
A sound to send chills through the mountains with flare
Freestyles on beaches, home sweet home with the mic
Meanwhile I'm reaching, greet the unknown in the light

Sonically lead to who found me in pairs
We are bound, we are bread, my brethren is there
See it's been awhile, breech the throne if I might
See me turn the dial, niche and moments bright

These are diamonds in rough, turntable needles in dark
Mind hunters giving up, enabling the people to start
Divine thunder rumbles, contemplating a spark
Designed to uncover who's playing the parts

We find emeralds in mud, soliloquies versed
Remind the unattainable abilities to surface
Blending in harmony our arts with a purpose
Azimuth, Lady Poetic- make sure you heard us!

LP's Lyrics From Dumb Cipher (With The El)

Me colé en la fiesta
Ken tried to make it, but I RSVPed instead, ya
La Poetica
De Norte de Sur America
Con mi amigo para siempre
Barbie's mas interesante
Esta es bestante
(Esta es bestante)
Internet connections, now connecting dots
Midwest to East coast affections, equated hot
Respect inside the lines, island's got the drop
Infectious energies, see- we won't stop

Speed demon to the extreme,
mueve su piernas to the beat
No need to be discrete,
Keep gazing through the air at this heat
See, in all fairness, we been worldwide from jumpstreet

Flip in like Phillipino, ma hal na mal kita

Come and rescue ya, like I'm Rasta
Roll you up and smoke you up, call me ma

mueve su piernas to the beat
mueve su piernas to the beat
Now keep moving ya feet
Keep movin ya feet

Dumb

“I can hear it now”
“you can hear it now”
“We can hear it now”
“He I can hear it now”
“dumb, da dumb”

Escucha nuestra cancion!

LP's G.O.A.T.E.D. Cypher Verse

Welcome to the Zou, where we welcome in the Lou
The tigers came to play, cardinals just flew their coup
We got emcees for hire- Blue Note: take the cue
With a tendency to breathe fire- what's she gonna do?

True makings of superstardom- and that's a fact
Tonight is the night we take real hip hop back
We gonna take some jabs, but we all givin' dap
After this show, Midwest goes up on the map

Sheer poetry by design, glowing under smoking lights
Hear me at an open mic, streaming, doin' shows worldwide
Waiting patiently for someone's bars to bend my mind
Ain't nothing but love but y'all shoulda had me headline

Collateral damage with a home court advantage
Fearless and unbranded, but this cameo ain't candid
Hear this on demand, while the motive is expanding
Gear up for the fans, all a part of game plannin'

Speaking of which, we got Evi da Prince
A-game making a name- you won't want to miss this
Yo- Don't you know how I roll with Canibus?
Somebody call Professor Griff while I omit explicits

Coming off as timid but the realest keep it vicious
Squad's hoppin' off the bus lookin' like a Temu wishlist
I'm just poppin' off- trust, this night's gon be exquisite
Now I think I need some Koolaid with my Red Hot Riplets

Brace yourselves, turn the page, headliners got it right
Lacing every beat in play- yo Josh B this one's tight!
Thank you all for joining us, tonight, on this plight
Lady Poetic on stage and I bow to you goodnight

Hip hop, hip hop, hip hop...
Whos' next?

LP's Lyrics For the Temple Heads Featuring Greydon Square Project

I'm a flight risk when I'm like this, minus nine stints of sleepless nights in
When I write this, I'm on an island, final highlights nestled right in
Bright and brisk, Arrival signing in the finest lines, finite vessels guiding,
Pining though pine needles on vinyls, wrestling hi-hats with their highness
Meteorites colliding on the very lines D flat happens to reside in
Feeling me right? Stop hiding. "But sir, the beacon's blinding"
See what you might, rock climbing through unheard, imperfect timing
Metabolites of opulent mind beams scream like sirens
Fire's friendly, fasten clasps and fashion frantic mind schemes
Entirely unnecessary, grasp your time and meet at high dream

Finally we're ready, avast the dash- the dashboard light's green
Cosmic clearance steadily, cast a squint from the planet's highbeams
Flyby's tethered mentally, match the print from the gambit's ninth scene
Temple Heads venture fast and Grand Unified's inviting
Neptune's silhouette's the venue, until then, we keep flying

Lift Up

Hoist up the trophy, raise up the gauntlet
Voices grow boldly, amazing and honest
Choices can only bring praise from the conscious
Noises will slowly rephrase a new promise

Lift up your spirits, each bar penned in splendor
Gift us with merit, each star sends a measure
Swift, tough and fearless, reach farther than ever
Winning- come cheer us, seek harder forever

Rooted in grace, polished by grit
Smoothed by the pace, obstacles, bit by bit
Soothing in taste, spotless with wit
Groove to the bass, populous witness this

Making our way towards the apex each day
Facing and paying it forward, we say
Obtaining the basics in more complex ways
Gaining what makes us a force, next in play

Emcees inspire to lift this up higher
Send me in rifts to run up and admire
Friendly, committed entire, breathe fire
Lend me your ears and hearts down to the wire

Irrespective of circumstances, don't you give up
Here we're reflective, take chances to lift up
We are collective, enhancing's a must
Give me life, give my lyrics, in hip Hop I trust

Lone Wolf Cry

This is all I know how to do

Give me a beat
Give me the paper and a pen

That's all I ever needed.
It's all I need right now.

Hear the Lone Wolf Cry
My exasperated sigh.
My defense mechanism is a slowly dying sentence.
It's with the utmost intention I only find suppression.

Friendships. Kinships, Relationships.
Hit then miss.
Ship has sailed
The lone wolf always prevails
All she needs besides herself is not one person
Hear my words strike a nerve, you know this is for certain
Heavy hearts hurting

Fully immersed in.

This Lone Wolf Cry...
It's piercing.

LP's Lyrics From "The Spitboss"

Intro voice: "People have stories"

LP: "We have a story to tell"

Intro voice: "You were there?"

LP: "We saw the whole thing.

And it went something like this..."

The date is engraved on a slate in a cave

Encased by the brave and chased by the depraved

At the foot of a maze overlooking Everglades

Where crooks bury blades and dig up hatchets to raise

Unfazed by taboo, I'm amazed that's it's you

Gaze through the muse, outdated pay per views

I'll trade you for clues, contemplate giving cues

Say, I stayed true, confiscating the ruse

We're better off in the shadows, *Ra's al Ghul* as our commander

Cleverly bathed in slander, the sender stood there, I just gather

Pretending to be fooled but rather- haphazard in a mind

standard
Prancing around old-school like a black panther with manners
Frantically shattered, behind the gallows, enamored
Practically standard, designing shallows with candor
Dastardly untame the clamor, knighted as passengers
Cast this creed in gold, foretold by student to master

Street Kings

(a DJ Galaxy Collabo)

Let's pass out some crowns

1990 memorizing MC Hammer
Idolizing MC Lyte and practicing my candor
Naughty by Nature, learning every bar, every letter
Gin n Juice, Salt n Pepa
Man it didn't get no better
Now it's 1993,
Watching Ice Cube and George Clinton on MTV
Bring some Pac into the mix
Man I never felt like this
Music speaking to my soul
It's A G-funk era
Funkdafied with a Blow Out Comb
1996 I'm coppin Sittin' on Chrome
From then til now Masta Ace holdin' the throne
It Was Written kept my head spinnin
ATLiens dropped- jackpot! Hip hop's winning
1998, my world's turned upside-down

My boy's like check out Second Round Knock Out
Then listen to Can-I-Bus from start to finish
Mind blown, IQ elevated from Bis' lyrics
Now the taste's refined, and the Technique Immortal
On a Celph Titled agenda to transport through portals
Moving from Biggie and Total
To the independent moguls
Writing my own rhymes now, and setting goals

With this body of rap, I say you Kings
With this body of rap, I say you Kings

Feeling like a Spottiottiedopalicious
Bumpin' Craig Mack, and hearing the word blowticious
No Vaseline was vicious
But Just For the Record be keeping me in stitches
Which is why the many types of styles to bump and up the hype
Keeps me sharp and mind so bright
DJ: bring this song to life

can you pop in the 8 track

rewind the tape
skip the cd?
Nah, baby, it's the vinyl for me

can you pop in the 8 track
rewind the tape
skip the cd?
Nah, baby, it's the vinyl for me

Pick up where I left off? Or fill in the gaps?
Cuz 1995 was one of the dopest years for rap
Y'all remember way back when
When you was 10
Street lights and fists fights
Watch them grow from Boys II Men
Fat Boys, Geto Boys, Lost Boyz
Organized or otherwise, make some noise
A voice for those without
From streets to clubs and Word of Mouf
From a Fisher Price boombox to seeing shows at Red
Rocks
A love like this never stops

Since 400 degreez we drop it like it's hot
If you got one shot, do not miss
One More Chance may last, make those move while they exist
Slick Rick James Brownsville to the Bone
Sample classics, make some magic, feel the tone

With this body of rap, I say you Kings
With this body of rap, I say you Kings

Now it's 97 and I'm watching the game evolve
Intrinsically for me, it's like a puzzle to solve
Elevatin' caliber, peep the pen game revolve
Seeing groups and duos droppin constants then dissolve
You learn a lot about yourself and how to operate
On the streets and in life from the music that we make
Feel me on this one, we got DJ Galaxy
and Lady Poetic rockin as the emcee

With this body of rap, I say you Kings
With this body of rap, I say you Kings

can you pop in the 8 track
rewind the tape
skip the cd?
Nah, baby, it's the vinyl for me

can you pop in the 8 track
rewind the tape
skip the cd?
Nah, baby, it's the vinyl for me

With this body
With this body of rap
With this body of rap I say
With this body of rap, I say you Kings

"For Oodie"

on behalf of Sylvia Robinson

Written by Lady Poetic

When I learned you were gone, I didn't know where to start
This hurts more than the blow to an unhealed heart
Every memory, every moment, shot past me like a dart
Never expecting this is how we would part

Now the void in my soul, starts growing old
Like we were supposed to, I'm holding my own
A loss like this, with words can't be told
The times we had were priceless, beautiful and bold

With you, I was alive, together we thrived
So without you, the pain drains me from the inside
At times I want to hide, or scream out with pride
For I love you my friend, that part will never die

You will be celebrated, and cherished often
Your legacy lives on, never forgotten
I will hold my head high, even when I must sigh

“See you later”, they say, because I can't say goodbye

A Poem for Tykee

(Written for my nephew)

Be strong, young man. You are raised in love.
Be brave, young man. I shall watch from above.
Be still, young man, when your heart is heavy.
Be fierce, young man, none of us were ready.
Be honorable, young man, I'm always by your side.
Be truthful, young man, wear our name with pride.
Be courageous, be fair
Even when I'm not there
Hold your head high, move with intention
My love is unconditional, and without question
Not even death can break our bond
I will love you from the sky, the grave, and beyond
Every moment we shared, is a moment to hold
Look back on these moments when you grow old
I'll be right here waiting, you are never alone
Stand tall, Tykee, it was my time to come home.
I love you in big ways, I love you in small ways,
I love you, young man, and I'll love you always.

LP's Lyrics From "Three Spirits"
(an XPreNN Collabo)

I be on my mad professor bit, hand over the tenure ship
Iron clad and diamond pressure, scanned over penmanship
Mad Men brand censored, damn- they glanced over this
The tad bit that I measured overflowin' to the graveyard shift

Decades of deliberations, found the perfect team
Makeshift laboratories in the basement, sound out certain schemes
Facelifts from the apothecaries, cased and drowned out screams
Face it- it's insane shit, boundless in dreams

Scribbled instructions woven into dope percussions
Meddling in the middle of the night, hopin' for something
Fiddled with the formula, we might come up from nothing
Whistled with no interruptions, hypotheses with gumption

Make this concoction breathe, etching the design

Debate options in secret, fetching more time
A creature's being created, venture my best guess
The feature's been anticipated, enter mad scientist....

LP's Lyrics From the Temple Heads Introduction

I don't want to make history- I want to make mythology
Rewrite the stars, be added to charts of cosmology
This is bar-ology, concoctions of the hardest oddities
Twenty thousand underneath a scholarly league

The friction is sizzling, black fires kindling;
The wisdom is missing, gnashing teeth entirely rippin' beats;
Meet and greet beneath the Temple, tappin' our feet;
Sweep you off cerebrally, sample snatchin' from Ivy Leagues

Clear the table, stack the deck, time to make way
We're capable- point, match and set, anchors away!
Channel Zero on the cable, call me collect
Panel Members- Mars to Naples, take your time to fact-check

Though never vindictive, our endeavor's superlative;
Asphyxiate the noise you heard so I can work with words

like this;
Murder it, lace it, grace it, bend it to 100 degrees and boomerang it;
Insane trips over Uniek Beats, break through ceilings from basements.

Awkward Cypher

I'm on one,
Too often
Hard to see through the mist so
Proceed with caution
Battling back to back in the back ad nauseam
Toss em up and 99 outta 100 its gone be a problem
Drum Line, just in time- Stomp the Yard wit em
Hard to find the rhythm, like ribbons blowing in the wind
With a microscopic, atomic vision
Whippin' through wormholes with writ precision
Slippery slopes when you open up to wisdom
Whimsically, assuredly
Enter in the attic door with a skeleton key
Melodramatic asthmatics on the line for me
Hellos so ecstatic, exuberant but silently
Flightless Bird, American Pie in the Sky type of dream
Primadonna with honor, Cloak N Dagger Avant gardener
Harvester of awkward bars, Spaceship to Mars
Stardust over scars, Russian Roulette with Fast Cars
Casino Cards

Carpe diem, paid per diem, Autumn leaves change in season
13 reasons
There's always been a hidden meaning
Look behind the skyline, clouds streaming
Beaming, glowing, is it showing
Alliances growing, pilot plan- all knowing
From Harlem to Dover, holding a 4 leaf clover
Charming and bold, you'll know when it's over
The graveyard shift goes on tour
Murkin melodies beneath the moon, plain and pure
A Liege, A Fuhrer
A Lady, Usurper
Turbulent trumpets with a baseline- I'd bump it
Run it up
Til the sun up
Bee sting Operation Phoenix
We up
We up
The graveyard shift goes on tour
Murkin melodies beneath the moon, plain and pure
A Liege, A Fuhrer

A Lady, Usurper

Turbulent trumpets with a baseline- I'd bump it

Run it up

Til the sun up

Bee sting Operation Phoenix

We up

We up

LP's Lyrics for the Boombox

(a Goon Rilla Collabo)

What up Goonrilla? Where you at cuddy...
Bout time we laced a track together, let's do this...

Back in '96, at the crib, taking hits
Freestyling, circle rhyming, we never missed
Goon Rilla, Reno, the Fonz and LP
Pass the invisible microphone to me
We spit to our own beat, or even off key
But kept the bars in circulation definitely
Sometimes for hours, clownin' with the lyrics
Leaving all the little gym shoes and shorties in hysterics
No warning, no merits, gully with the spirits
Fast forward to present day and you can finally hear us
Mirror mirror this, casting shadows, catching heat
Molding such magnificence, bold now with the beat
Persistent with the rhymes schemes, no need to compete
Two of the dopest emcee cousins you will ever meet
From then to now, let's show em how we coming prepared
From the Lac to the Bay, baby we ain't never cared!

Cassette tapes to CDs, stolen players, memories
Renig on the spades and we'll see a tragedy
Blood or water, no matter, we been family
Cracking jokes, passin smokes, living candidly
Set up the bones, pour the drinks, we in the zone
May be a minute to get in it but we set the tone
A chip off the old block but we keepin it cool
From the Circle up to Green Bay we was actin a fool
Cash Money, Scarface, Pac and all the old school
Set by certain standards, abide by certain rules
Goon in the building with the freshest drip and dopest hair
I'm fairly certain, heads still turning, bygones beware

Wack DJs

(a DJ Galaxy Collabo)

Ayo I'm feeling this already
I like the way you scratch
I heard you got them turntables,
Tossin' on those throwbacks
First of all I field no fables
Flossin' with the Golden Era tracks

I'm only housing one complaint-
Let me spit a bar or two on that
“Start, stop, press play”
No fade to the next jam- can you explain that?!
There's more elements to the art
Now walk with me through time to way back (way back)

Not so long ago, August of '73
Bronx, New York, heat radiating off the concrete
It's a party over on Sedgwick, hosted by Cindy
Her big brother Kool Herc gone DJ and emcee
Here come the breaks! The Merry Go Round!

The birth of hip hop is going down
Now all around town, b-boys and girls
Expressing themselves, escaping to a Different World

Ayo I'm feeling this already
I like the way you scratch
I heard you got them turntables,
Tossin' on those throwbacks
First of all I field no fables
Flossin' with the Golden Era tracks

Keep it going now, it's 50 years later
Whether you a listener, cultivator or stargazer
Note the real facets that go into mixing flavor
It's more than just a playlist- a DJ's not a party favor!
But do me a favor, next time you listen
It's more than just an emcee spittin,
More than vinyls moving underneath a pin- that's a given
More than stacking same track after track, basic business

Ayo I'm feeling this already
I like the way you scratch

I heard you got them turntables,
Tossin' on those throwbacks
First of all I field no fables
Flossin' with the Golden Era tracks

Now walk with me through time to way back (way back)...

Dead Woman Bars Vol. 1

Drudged up from the dungeon, coughin' concrete dust
Mustered up from coffins, it's not often, still in touch
From the womb to the tomb and every season between
Impending tombs and haunting tunes gives reasons
foreseen

Dead woman walking, but she got those bars
I sense someone stalking, they're not very far
I'm breaking bad with the Ironclads-men
Forsaking all I had- too many irons in the fire, man!

Ions circling above like buzzards, it's strange
Aeons hurl for one another- death won't die estranged
Calling out an S.O.S. as I lurk through the bayous
Falling down like pessimists, working to find you

Stalling, hoarding consciousness, searching to guide you
Drawing, storyboarding, lest it hurts to undermine you
I'm behind you, beside you, resurrect the charge
Design true, and mind you, it's Dead Woman Bars

Dead Woman Bars Vol 2

From the moment of the explosion, to a house gone up in flames
Plunging from three stories, blackened lungs but spared my brains
Writhing through the snow in pain, pictures burned, melted frames
I saved my soul, this I know, but looking back it's a shame

Soot filled nostrils, singed eyelashes
Riding hostile, cringed in ambulances
Flirted with death but saved the last dances
It hurt but I'm rebirthed and snatching up chances

No blame, no pity- I do this for the city
For the pengame and the music, keepin' my nails gritty
If I weren't half dead, you might consider me pretty
I 'll be grinding instead, sometimes thug, sometimes silly

Still just one of the guys, nothing savvy or heroic
Took my foot out the grave, grabbed the mic and provoked

it

This is our style, ink to page, now we chose it

Dead Woman Bars, Volume 2- how appropriate!!

Dead Woman Bars Vol. 3

Overprepared and unsung from the views
Bird's eye and midcry, stung and subdued
Only what's shared and among certain clues
The third try of nine lives, sprung from a muse

The rhymes are a riddle entwined within stanzas
Finding the skills the divine would demand of us
Designing the will to defy missing manners
Implying the time will unwind, whisking past us

I stared through the treetops, suspended in air
Layered beats of hip hop, to mend and repair
The mare with the horn atop, bending the snares
So fair and forlorn, we stopped sending in pairs

I twisted together a pattern from Mars
Snooze til you hit Saturn, then watch from afar
If you missed it, then gather the last of the falling stars
Refusing to shatter, made of Dead Woman Bars

Dead Woman Bars Vol. 4

Barred from the charts ‘fore I even applied
Hardened from scars torn by talons in skies
Pardoned by stars who’ve sworn me to try
Sharpened by guards now adorning the prize

Left for lions
Climbing up fence posts planted by neighbors
Rhyming so intense, evaporated from papers
Timings immense, smoke enchanted by vapors
Finding regrets most from actions unfavored

Tapered down doses, albeit consuming
Word around town just to see it amusing
Wait for the crowns as we toast to this moving
Spared and grounded, must be in what I’m choosing

Ten thousand lines running rampant up here
Send down the miners, gunning and gassing in fear
Pretend there’s no priors, lunging at laughing steers
We mend and inspire, stunned and outlasted peers

Dead Woman Bars Vol. 5

I've walked down streets where my skin tone's forbidden
Gawked at then greeted when I'm dope with the writtens
Talked about sounds leading hope toward ambition
Balked at the men who deleted known visions

Since it's been given- a wordsmith, a gift
Horses run wild, ya but I'm here for this
Glimpse in misgivings, merciless fits
Consortiums unfiled, the innocent drifts

Sidewalk serenades follow moonlit reasons
My mind stalks pages hollowed by meanings
Defined talks made us bellow at the meetings
Grind, walk the walk, mellow and seasoned

I've already apexed, any more is a bonus
Steady and patient, making more for the chosen
Against any grain, perplexing and focused
Dead woman, 'mayne', raise the bar, she has spoken

Dead Woman Bars Vol. 6

Flat liners glide between wormholes in the matrix
Backslide through time, burning souls into spaces
Providing the signs to earn goals through the ages
Fractions entwined, yearning most for the basics

A simple sixteen, the function to breathe
A riddle underneath, it's a junction where to meet
The grid lies beneath, it's something just to see
Witness the queens, we're hunting your breed

Dead woman bars, the 6th installation
From the red planet Mars to the dankest of basements
Bred from the hardest emcee compilations
Embedded in part in the mixers amazement

Brave yet buried, still living the dream
Maimed and daring, instilling serene
From the grave, records blaring, willful unseen
Estranged from uncaring, the guild waits for me

Dead Woman Bars Vol. 7

I'm from the Temple; This is heavy mental
Heaven-sent, you know; But As Above, So Below
This is HBO at the Gallows
The atmosphere is hallowed, like your temperament, it's shallow

Mud-plastered gears get stuck in limbo and below, above the mantle
Fanatical, obsessive, but the lyrics get impressive
Take a sabbatical in discretion, then bring the selection
Out of habit you'll be stressing when the premise gets interesting

Missing the last page of the chapter's climatic ending
My gravestone is dusty and the epitaph's pretending
Say it ain't so-the cinematic script is testing.
Blame it on the cold, or the amusement just for jesting

Let's grow through the music, bring me back to life, this is it

Save my soul when it's intrusive, point out my deficits
Give me grace, patience, hit the criticism, when it fits.
Tip toe through the tulips while I'm pushin' daisies into
print

Dead Woman Bars Vol. 8

It's midnight, in Miami, I'm rollin up my Vice
Escaping from the grave? Yeah you gonna pay the price
Them pavements I was chasing? They crumbled on me twice
The insight is outstanding, running under Northern Lights

Underneath a lunar eclipse I brought you certain gifts
You'll understand it one day, there was magic in the mix
Now the thunder's clapping, lighting strikes to highlight perfect riffs
Wondering what's been happening as the sax blows me a kiss

Floating like an alto right above soprano's hips
Swaying to the bassline, replay this with all my hits
Sunsets in the rear view, gears about to shift
Migrate where the sun still shines, no promises

Vintage in the image when it's hidden in plain sight
Sentences will scrimmage just before they say goodnight

Revered in any season, brain is blooming, just you wait
Nearly was high treason, playing Dead Woman Bars Vol. 8

Dead Woman Bars Vol. 9

There will come a time
And place
Where you'll recognize my voice
And recognize my face

Until then...
I keep experimenting
Writing and grinding,
It's imperative, you see
A steady constant when you find me

I might kick one for the masses, but this here's for the chambers
A little sick but take my chances, fear not for then, danger
Brick by brick, keep it on lock, cheers from perfect strangers
Witty when I ought not, heated convos with debaters

There's no window for opportunity where I'm coming from

I stay on the move, keep up with the groove, show my face as seldom as I want
Spit one from the crates, twenty years young
Then jump on the radio station, hear the latest one get spun

This is an intricate journey, boundless and ever demanding
I'll be known as one of the underground kings by the time my lungs stop expanding
Time be at my mercy, they haven't found me, but I'm ready
Hungry, but not thirsty, havoc- wreaking, guess who sent me?

I'm spitboss kin, CC fam, the brethren got me covered
Upheld in the highest lights when we mention one another
New to you, an up and comer, but I'm from another time
Temple of Bars, represent, this is Dead Woman Bars Vol. 9

Dead Woman Bars Vol. 10

Hello my friends.
What have we here?
Dead Woman Bars
Vol. 10

I bust out of the broken gates outside the town saloon
I heard there'll be a duel tomorrow, same place at high noon
I must be out my goddamn mind, that's coming up too soon
Plus I left my pistol in the brothel, man I'll be ruined

Maybe I should steal a horse, start robbing coach and carriage
We could improvise of course, it'd be the dopest marriage
Set off for the sunset when the weather's at it's fairest
Me and my finest steed, tabooed times to cherish

The stakes were a little high at that last hand of poker
Breaking off three of a kind, the Royal Flush left me broker
Ace of diamonds up his sleeve, under my foot's a joker
I begged and pleaded but they're coming for this midnight

toker

Now there's a couple hours, place a bet or get revenge
Sirens at the towers, takes the wildest to avenge
My promise lies in the mountains, sign with smoke signals
at the bend
Is my voice growing louder yet with Dead Woman Bars
Volume 10?

Kicks

Oooh, I like those kicks! Those are fly. Goes with your
drip. Yeah, you on fire
Oooh, I like those kicks! Those are fly. Goes with your
drip. Yeah, you on fire

You remember back in the day, we wore them new Jordans,
and Reebox?
Copped the Nike Cortez with them footsie socks
Sported the pumas, started rumors by the lockers
Jordache shorts and Vans, skating by with the high tops on

First to get the latest Filas, then bump some Leschea
Heard that New Masta Ace? Throw my boots on- store's a
mile away
Snatching up new vinyls, lacing up my pair of BK Knights
With the triple laces, goodness gracious they got lights!

Timbalands in the winter, never got into those Uggs
Thought about some red bottoms but I'm still a thug
Keep my toesies cozy with a pair of brand new pair of

slippers
Maybe rock the leather with the side frays and a zipper

Anytime I rock those K- Swiss, fellas bumpin' my fist
Standing in line at a concert, poppin off in these Converse
Hope nothing spills upon my new white trainers,
I'm trying to Stay on point like Stacy Adams

Oooh, I like those kicks! Those are fly. Goes with your drip. Yeah, you on fire
Oooh, I like those kicks! Those are fly. Goes with your drip. Yeah, you on fire

I'm trying to keep this new pair clean,
Brush em wit a toothbrush, bleach the laces, 'na mean?
Velcro, cleats, Bobos, neat, house shoes rock the bells,
New Chuck Taylor's for the street, do live and tell

Tap shoes in the closet, combat boots on a deposit
DCs when I'm stompin all around in the mosh pit
Feel the need to set the vibe and tie it to the outfit
Penny loafers wit the three piece suit, chillin' in the office

Spittin about what's on your feet, heard you runnin' with those Brooks
New Balance prevents them callous, stuntin with the looks
Still a fan- shell toe Adidas, rock em with my joggers
Got the knock off crocs when I kayak through the marshes

Got 6 inch stilletos when I'm feeling kinda feisty
Pimpin alligator shoes, cigar lit with a match- remind me
What time is we clubbin'? got some Pro Wings for my fit
Finest when I'm barefoot in the kitchen , but this one's about the Kicks...

Oooh, I like those kicks! Those are fly. Goes with your drip. Yeah, you on fire
Oooh, I like those kicks! Those are fly. Goes with your drip. Yeah, you on fire

Ay. Them some nice kicks you got on though...

Quartz Trip
(an Azimuth Collabo)

This is from an ultra-classified, sanctified mind
Spun into dendrites, suspended in time
Silver lined, demystified, defunded signs
Desensitized and sprung into unsung crimes

Obtunded from inner monologues, making faux pas
Redundant prayers in synagogues, forsaking what was
Drummed up by ministers, chasing the slugs
Stunts layered sinister, facing shots mugged

A blip in the Quartz trip, time folds in wrinkles
A drip from the gauntlet last sipped, surface rippled
Ripped from remorse with the signatures crinkled
Stripped from the North with a transport so simple

I'm Stalin in the Soviet to make Germanic advances
Fallin for the Laureate to break ecstatic trances
Pausing for the poets with phonetic enhancements
Cause and effect for emphatic detachments

This is the Quartz trip, defunded memory lane
The sorta beat that rips and plunges into your brain
Thought patterns scattered then realigned again
Lost matter captured, the mind's mine my friends

Glossed over manuscripts scribbled by the one
Embossed over tablets made brittle by the sun
Gawked over fascists riddled with puns
Stalked older catchments, (little) by little undone

Pinches of metal, a dash of eccentric
Since it all settled, the clash is extensive
Trippin on pedals, gassed and left pensive
Glitchin' through Quartz trips, fractured, insensitive

Bumped my machinehead, Tiger's Eye glows
Jumped with the freeman, higher she rose
Slummed it with millionaires, Empire grows
Runnin' without a care, walk wires 'round globes

My putamen's emaciated, ultimate crash

Reframe the unsatiated, fulminate pasts
The game's unappreciated, culprits amass
Remember my name, once great, once The Last

This is the Quartz trip, defunded memory lane
The sorta beat that rips and plunges into your brain
Thought patterns scattered then realigned again
Lost matter captured, the mind's mine my friends

Squeezing through portals in east Puerto Rico
Teasing the mortals while reaching for these goals
Breezing through courseloads, least of what's been told
Seizing each moment to meet what's been foretold

Bolder, still restless, navigating terrains
Turmoil infesting the best of the brains
Furloughed from guessing creations insane
Smoldering lanes from a trail gone ablaze

Chillin in the spaces between piano keys
Stealing the bases unseen by families
Fingertips braced secretly in lucid dreams

Quartz Trips extorted beneath fantasies

Pleasantries, escapades, all in exchange
Memories vacated, Polaroids fade
Sensories blanketed, in golden fields laid
Preparatory stories, in full we were paid

This is the Quartz trip, defunded memory lane
The sorta beat that rips and plunges into your brain
Thought patterns scattered then realigned again
Lost matter captured, the mind's mine my friends

Afterward

Shout out to you for reading my poetry and lyric book! I hope it was well received. I put special thought and attention into every line (or bar), and as you may or may not have noticed, there are many metaphors and Easter Eggs to be appreciated throughout!

Writing is something I feel I was born to do, and it has come to me in many forms over the years, whether in poems, song lyrics, books, articles or more.

May you find the creative spirit in yourself and keep reading, glowing and growing!

Many thanks for the support and trust in keeping the written word and hip hop alive and well.

Cheers!

-LP

www.ingramcontent.com/pod-product-compliance
Lightning Source LLC
LaVergne TN
LVHW020626100826
845148LV00012B/2073

* 9 7 9 8 9 8 8 0 2 9 7 3 1 *